# Cyber Bullying:

# Why and How Cyber Bullies Operate

By

Adetutu Ijose

Published By:

Jointheirs Publishing

JP

Cyber Bullying:
Why and How Cyber Bullies Operate

Jointheirs Publishing
Jointheirs Activities Incorporated
www.jointheirspublishing.com

ISBN – 1-46100-367-9

EAN – 978-1-46100-367-0

Printed in the United States of America

# CYBER BULLYING:

# WHY AND HOW CYBER BULLIES OPERATE

# *An Important Caution*

The advice given in *Cyber Bullying* is based on an understanding of the effects of computer use on human behavior gained when I suffered life threatening consequences of computer use and began to understand the human code of existence from studying the human machine user manual we call the Bible or Scriptures.

I have applied this understanding to the issues affecting teenagers and the behavioral issues they are experiencing in the technological age as their lives revolve around computers and computer devices all day This book is informational and is a guide that contains both advice and instructions. It is essential that you read the entire book carefully and that any decision you make be discussed with your physician and parents if you are a teenager as well as school authorities or any other person of authority in your life before proceeding.

If you are a parent or other adult reading this book, please take time to discuss with your child and get their perspective on things. Also discuss with your child's physician and school authorities to get their perspective on your child regardless of whether they are being bullied or the bully or an observer to the act of bullying.

If you are a teenager, this book is not meant to replace the advice of parents or the service of a health care provider who knows you personally. An essential element of taking responsibility for your life and health is having a good relationship with your parents and other persons in authority over you.

If you are an adult, having regular conversations with your teenager, giving advise and being on top of whatever is going on around them is important as well as getting them regular checkups and working in partnership with medical professionals and counselors.

If you or if you are a parent, your child is under treatment for any computer-related behavioral disorder or if you suspect you might need such care, you must discuss any insight you gain from this book with your doctor before starting.

# *Table of Contents*

# Chapter 1
## *Introduction*

This book is intended to be a health and lifestyle help for teenagers and the adults who are in authority over them at home and in school as well as their care giver and anyone who is in charge of making policies that affect teenagers.

What it will do is provide information to enable the reader understand the biological issues behind the teenage behavior of cyber bullying. It will also shed light on why some adult indulge in taking on the character of teenagers on the computer with the aim of cyber bullying.

It will assist in taking decisions about how to help teenagers have a better understanding of why they are behaving the way they are and assist in establishing guidance for responsible computer use at home and at school which will reduce the tendency for bullying.

It is important to remember that any guidelines established must be followed through to be successful. It is my hope that as people read this book they will better understand the limitations that have been put in place by our maker in nature to prevent us from hurting ourselves and learn to operate within those boundaries to avoid self destructive actions.

For more detailed reading about the health and behavioral effects of computer use and how to minimize them, please get hold of my other books in print and in ebook version available amazon.com and other online store. You may also want to visit my website www.foodsthathealdaily.com .

The understanding gained from this book will assist individuals in identifying the various behavioral and health-related changes that are going on in their lives as a result of the effect of computer-related activities on the brain, nerves, muscles, and various organs of their bodies. These effects are the consequence of the unnatural nature of the computer-use environment on our bodies. For example, we do not look directly at the sun our natural coded light for reading to read but we look directly at the computer light to read creating unnatural stresses in our body's system it was not designed for.

This book could also assist in communicating during discussions with physicians to avoid being misdiagnosed as psychotic if other behavioral issues as a result of excessive computer exposure accompany bullying or a victim's emotional stress.

In this book, I am trying to shed light on the health problems that are inherent in computer use when proper preventative measures are not put in place to protect the human machine.

This book and its content is only a guide, and individual situations will definitely vary.

# Chapter 2
## *Cyber Bullying*

In years past before the Internet age, being teased in school and learning to stand up for yourself and others was viewed as a normal part of growing up and it never resulted in permanent damage. This was probably because in those days it was limited to school time and it was more of teasing if you were a girl and learning how to defend yourself if you were a boy i.e. part of the learning experience.

It is a well known fact that the teenage brain is in the developmental stage and is prone to excessive excitement and is not totally capable of understand the full ramifications of personal action. Unfortunately for the teenager, we are now in the technology age, which means constant exposure to artificial light from computers and computer devices such as ipads, ipods, video games, cell phones with texting capabilities and so on that is an additional stress to the stress of the hyper activity of growing up. This poses a lot of challenges to the developing brain and mind

The computer and most especially the internet and the impersonal cyber world may seem like a world where one does not have to take responsibility for one's actions especially to the developing excitable teenage mind. It can also seem to be one where one can get away with anything and avoid being caught, which can make the temptation to experiment with all kinds of dark behavior to see how others would react rather overpowering. This becomes more tempting for any teenager wanting to maintain popularity and show off to others.

Indeed much as the computer and its devices such as blackberries, ipads, ipods and so on have been very useful in our modern day lives and have indeed become indispensable to our daily lives, there are also some negative consequences of its advent one of which is cyber bullying. This is the art of posting adversarial or negative comments about others on their social website pages or by sending negative hurtful emails and/or text messages with the intent of inflicting emotional pain.

What makes it even more tempting is that you do not see the person you are bullying making it easy to become merciless since there are no screams and tears to weaken the evil resolve of the bully. All this has made what used to be harmless teasing to evolve into something very dark. It is no longer the harmless character-building phase it used to be. It has now become the opposite, the character-destroying phase of life that leaves a lifetime scar for survivors.

The Internet has been a very effective medium for achieving this dark desire in bullies as one's emotions and not their physical strength is what is employed in computer use. You cannot have a physical fight on the Internet but you can have an emotional one and the stronger person wins just as it would be if there was a fight involving physical muscles.

Consequently when a child is attacked by a lot of their peers online it is just as it would be if a gang of kids physically beat up a child. The pain in this case is emotional bruises and cuts and not physical bruises and broken bones

In increasing number of bullying cases reported in the news there is a loss of life as teenagers take their own lives rather than continue being bullied or face the sneers from their peers. They are at an age when taunts seem so devastating and they have not yet built the thick skin that is developed from experience and brain coping system development. Suicide rates are up. The daily news is full of suicide and attempted suicide as well as mental issues arising in teens as a result of cyber bullying.

There has been many reasons given for this new phenomenon however no one is really looking at the biochemical effect of the exposure of the developing brain to excessive artificial electromagnetic fields inherent in computer use.

In addition there is the issue of a high level of violent computer games available to children making them wired for violence and bullying. The fact is that many of these video games involve a lot of bullying.

After all, with computer games, the characters even if they die are always there the next time they play. They never die permanently. Once the target is used to replace the video game character, there is no limit to how much bullying can be vented on the target by the bully. In his or her mind, it is only a game.

When adults decide to take on the role of kids and bully, they regress to the level of kids even if they have children of their own. They and their victims become characters in a video game and or their victims become the enemies they had when they were children and they deal out as much punishment as they can, forgetting they are adults. The biochemical depletions caused by computer light and the absence of human contact makes it easy for them to become detached and forget they are adults dealing with kids.

Once this mode sets in, it becomes difficult to get out of unless there is a shock treatment, which is what happens when the victim commits suicide or does something destructive for example. That is what wakes these adults up at which point it is usually too late.

My advice is never bully. Remember you are not fully emotionally balanced when on the computer. The computer use environment is one of inherent chemical and electrical imbalances. The light is lifeless and cannot stimulate your brain to produce the biochemicals you need to be balanced and make totally rational decisions. It is easy to lose control and get carried away as you are not fully balanced. Do not think you are in control of your emotions even if it seems you are. The fact that you are bullying a kid and enjoying it is evidence of the fact that an imbalance has set in and you have lost control.

Once you start on the irrational (bully) end you do not have the capability to rebalance until you leave that environment and get yourself rebalanced which most people do not do. Over time the imbalance becomes deeper and deeper and can only be reversed by a shock treatment.

It becomes a high much like one gets from alcohol and the bully begins to crave the fix of control, anonymity and deception unable to fully grasp the reality of their actions much like someone drunk from alcohol. Nerve messaging biochemicals called neurotransmitters such as dopamine are heavily depleted by computer use just as with alcohol and psychedelic drug use. Connection with reality recedes and getting the high is the only consideration.

On the victim's side, because of the depleting effect of the artificial light on the biochemicals like GABA and Serotonin (neurotransmitters that help to calm us down), emails and comments received from computer related sources are more devastating on our emotions.

Children are very prone to being affected, because as we have learned in this book, they are not fully matured emotionally and their brains are not fully developed. The biochemicals that help us in fully understanding our actions in a logical rather than emotional way is not in full production yet because this is the nurturing period.

This is when we are naturally supposed to get our sense of direction from our parents and others in authority over us. We learn to follow instructions and to relate to others in a constructive way under the guidance of our parents and guardians.

This makes this period in life the most vulnerable as the desire to be liked trumps all others. Everything is looked at from an emotional prism. This is also the period when we learn to curb negative emotions and we are taught the virtue of doing so.

And as we have said, because the Internet can provide anonymity, there is a temptation for people to decide not to curb their negative emotions because they believe they will not be caught. The effect of the toxic artificial light and chemicals that reflect from computer screens on our biochemical balance make things seem far removed from reality.

It is easy especially for kids since their brains are not fully developed and because they see many things from the angle of characters they read about in books, watch on the television and play with in video games to regard people they deal with like the characters in the computer games they play.

This dehumanizes others in their eyes making it difficult for the bully to place himself or herself in the place of the person on the receiving end or to relate to the emotions of their victims.

Because the computer related world is not real, the victim is unable to point to a human person to complain about and it usually takes a parent's vigilance to know something is wrong.

In a normal visual relationship you can read a person's body language and inaudible words can be spoken to convey feelings. The medium of computer-connected conversation does not allow this form of expression. We are visual creatures and we hear audibly and inaudibly every time we are with others and consequently hear from them many things they do not say audibly and are able to reach a more accurate conclusion about what they are saying.

Without this form of communication our understanding of others is incomplete and our understanding of what they are saying is also incomplete and so we reach conclusions about their intentions that may be way off from reality.

This is the problem with computer-based conversations. It is not complete.

As I have written in chapter 1, my advice to parents is that they educate their kids about the fact that when they are on the computer they should try to remember that human beings are different from video game characters

If your child is on the receiving end help them realize that the relationship is not real because it is not directly human-to-human but via a lifeless environment that cannot convey emotions. Consequently what they think they perceive may not be real but a figment of the imagination.

Help your children to stay grounded and not get carried away by what they think is the emotion being directed at them as emotions cannot be passed through the lifeless medium of the computer.

Help them to understand that there is an intermediary the computer that is unfortunately lifeless and cannot help them in reporting online issues to their parents or in getting them help. Parents should educate their children on all this. The medium of contact is not real and can be made to be anything a person wants it to be.

If you are a bully remember, the video game is make belief but when humans die it is final. The real world is finite it is not unlimited like computer virtual life.

Another advice to parents - monitor your child's activity on the computer. If they make friends, encourage them to ask to talk to these friends on the phone get to talk to the kids too and their parents and also get them to meet these friends physically under your supervision and never alone to ensure they are who they say they are. Remember the computer use environment is one of chemical and electrical imbalances that affect the ability to make sound judgmental decisions.

Children may seem to need privacy but when someone is constantly subject to the imbalances inherent in computer use it becomes difficult to separate reality from fiction and to discern when one stops and the other begins. Parental involvement especially with a child who spends long hours in a computer based relationship will save you future sorrow. Never let your children spend too long on the computer, the longer they are there the more their biochemical imbalance becomes and the more vulnerable or vicious they become depending on the bent of their imbalance.

# Chapter 3
## *Summary and Conclusion*

I hope I have helped you to gain a better understanding of cyber bullying by providing a glimpse into the inner secret working of the brain and mindset of both the bully and the victim. I hope this insight has provided you with some tips to enable you understand yourself or your child better.

Human mental health and behavior depend on the balance of biochemicals in our brain, depletion and resultant imbalances from computer use especially of those that calm us down resulting in over activation of excitative ones like Dopamine, could result in various behavioral and mental issues that our teens and others may otherwise not get involved in with dire consequences.

The combination of emotional stress and biochemical depletions from computer use could result in bullied children coming up with various issues such as symptoms that resemble depression

It is easy, for many of these behavioral problems arising from overexposure of the developing mind to artificial electromagnetic fields their brains are unable to cope with, to become misdiagnosed as psychotic problems and treated with high power drugs with dire consequences.

These behavioral issues if well understood could actually be solved with some lifestyle changes A pharmacist friend of mine told me if you are not psychotic and take psychotic drugs you would become psychotic so instead of one problem we could unnecessarily have 2 with neither being resolved

Reduced sleep/rest time for repair and growth as a result of going from desktop/laptop to ipads and iphone and video games and texting all day- coupled with reduction in melatonin production due to long hours and lack of sunlight exposure, is a recipe for behavioral issues and hyper excitation that could make children get into risky behavior such as cyber bullying as they burn up inhibitor biochemicals that could otherwise help them to take more rational actions.

Then there is the danger of losing communication skills resulting in children making themselves even more prone to being victims or bullies unable to understand the seriousness of their online activities.

Computer dependent communication as we have learned in chapter 2 is incomplete and is based on the perception of the individual with regards to the emotions being expressed and not reality, as emotions cannot be passed on through the lifeless computer. Too much dependence on this kind of controlled communication could make it difficult for individuals to handle real life conversation, as these will not be within their control.

Cyber bullying may be especially troublesome for people who are on video games all the time as many of these games involve a lot of bullying and violence under the influence of overproduced excitative neurotransmitters like dopamine. Since no one is fully in control of himself or herself when on the computer due to all the various neurotransmitter depletions, it is easy for these individuals to lapse into the video game experience and replace the person on the other end with video game character and exert as much bullying as if it was a video game.

In the case of virtual entrapment, now we have people having virtual families houses and so on that are just the way they want and this could result in inability to handle real life i.e. dehumanization of the living experience and losing control to lifeless computers making this kind of person more susceptible to online emotional manipulation

Technology makes parenting that more difficult especially at a time when financial stress means leaving children on their own for long periods but there is no choice if we are to help our children and avoid heartaches for ourselves. They need closer monitoring. Their developing brains cannot really handle the additional stress of relentless computer use without enough safeguards as is happening today. Hence we have ever-increasing occurrences of behavioral and other developmental issues.

Children you need help even if you think you do not, your brains are still developing and science tells us the part that enables you to fully grasp the consequence of your actions is the last to fully develop and this happens fully anytime after forty which is why when we get to that magical age we suddenly realize what we have been doing and cannot understand why we were so crazy at a younger age. That is why we need the guidance of parents. Let them help you.

# Note To The Reader:

## About the author:

Adetutu Ijose, is a technology and accounting professional with over 25 years of intensive computer use exposure who suffered life threatening computer related health conditions the doctors could neither diagnose not treat. In desperation and with a good knowledge of codes and how they work she studied the human computer user manual we call the Bible until she was able to understand why and how the computer hurts our body's system as well as the preventative and repair kits placed in nature by our maker.

She also gained an understanding of how computer use results in many behavioral issues she noticed had become prevalent in the global society since the advent of the computer and the internet such as cyber bullying, depression, suicides and so on especially amongst teens.

She is now passing on her understanding about computer use induced issues including cyber bullying, various other behavioral and mental issues as well as issues such as cancer, carpel tunnel syndrome eye issues and so on to everyone so others can receive help and avoid preventable devastating consequences of computer use.

Adetutu Ijose is a speaker on the subject of computer use induced health conditions. She is also a contributor to several online article websites and blogs including content sites associatedcontent.com and examiner.com. She has also been interviewed on radio.

To schedule a speaking engagement or interview with the author, please contact Adetutu Ijose at http://www.foodsthathealdaily.com.

For Adetutu Ijose's online press kit or for press releases and other media matters, please go to http://lessosilearnedthehardway.com/AdetutuIjoseMediaPressKit.aspx

Discover other titles by Adetutu Ijose to help you better understand responsible computer use and how computer use affect us all as well as what we need to do to prevent and manage these issues at www.foodsthathealydaily.com, www.amazon.com and other online stores. Ebook versions of this and other books by Adetutu Ijose are available at amazon.com, Barnes and Nobles, Smashword.com and other ebook stores

Connect with Adetutu Ijose Online:
Facebook: http://www.facebook.com/home.php

# INDEX

## A

## B

## C

# D

Deception, 9
Dehumanizes, 11
Desktop/laptop, 15
Developmental, 16
Dopamine, 9,14,15
Drugs, 14

# E

Electrical, 9,12
EEectromagnetic fields, 8, 14
Emails, 7,10
Emotional, 7, 9, 10, 14, 16
Emotional stress, 5, 14
Emotions, 7, 9, 10, 11, 12, 15
Enemies, 8
Environment, 5, 7, 9, 12
Evil, 7
Excitable, 6
Excitement, 6
Experiment, 6
Exposure, 5, 6, 8, 14, 15, 17

# G

GABA, 9
Guidance, 4, 10, 16
Guide, 1, 5

# H

Health, 1, 4, 5, 14, 17
Human, 1, 5, 8, 11, 12, 14, 17,
Human machine, 1, 5